$3 + 3 = 6$

$4 + 3 = 7$

$4 + 4 = 8$

$5 + 4 = 9$

$5 + 5 = 10$

First published in 1975.
This edition published by HarperCollins Publishers Ltd in 2001

3 5 7 9 10 8 6 4 2

ISBN: 0 00 711147 9

The HarperCollins website address is: www.fireandwater.com

Printed in Thailand

Richard Scarry
Best Counting Book Ever

Collins

An imprint of HarperCollinsPublishers

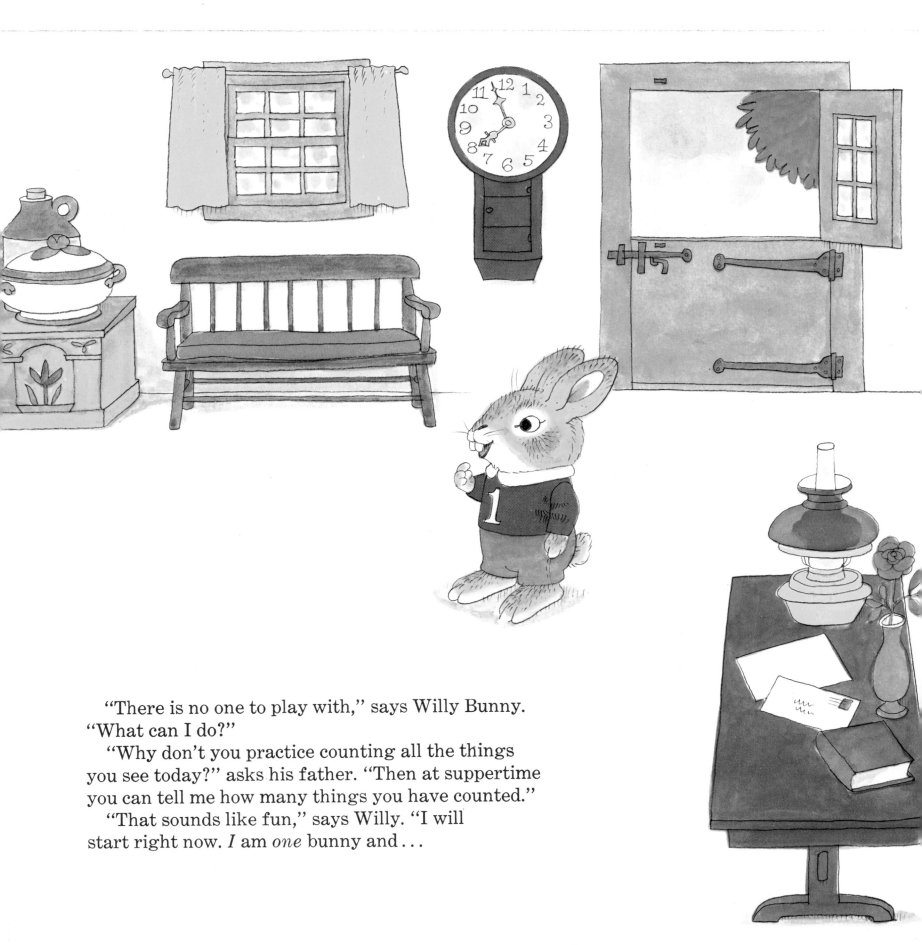

"There is no one to play with," says Willy Bunny. "What can I do?"

"Why don't you practice counting all the things you see today?" asks his father. "Then at suppertime you can tell me how many things you have counted."

"That sounds like fun," says Willy. "I will start right now. *I* am *one* bunny and . . .

1 one

"Oh, look! Here comes Sally Bunny.
One bunny and one bunny make two bunnies."
Both bunnies have two eyes, two hands, two feet,
and two long ears.

2 two

One mother and one father
make two parents.
Two fried eggs make a good
breakfast for Daddy.
Can you count two of
anything else?

3 three

Willy and Sally go outside to play.
Along comes their friend, Freddy Bunny.
Two bunnies and one bunny make three bunnies.
How many wheels are on Freddy's tricycle?
That's right! There are three wheels.

"Look at the three trucks," says Willy.
"One is big and two are small."

4 four

Here comes Flossie Bunny with her wagon.
Three bunnies and one bunny make four bunnies.
Now there are two girl bunnies and two boy bunnies.
Flossie has brought four apples in her
four-wheeled wagon for everyone to share.

Four mouse buses go down the street.
Two are yellow and two are red.

5 five

Beep-beep. Here comes Joey on his go-cart.
That makes five bunnies. Four were here already,
and one more makes five.

Four of the bunnies hear
their mothers calling them home.
Four bunnies go home.
That leaves just one bunny—Willy.
But Willy doesn't mind being alone.
He still has lots of things to count.
He sees five racing cars.

"One, two, three, four,
five," he counts.

6 six

Ding! Ding! Ding!   Ding! Ding! Ding!
Five fire engines and a fire chief's car
are speeding down the street.
That makes six in the fleet.
Three have ladders. Three do not.
Five are red, and one is white.
Where is the fire?

7 seven

The fire must be in the Cat family's farmhouse.
Seven cats are running out of the house.
Five are dressed and ready for school.
The other two are a mother and a baby.

8 eight

The fire is in Mother Cat's oven,
where she is baking eight pies.
Five pies are burned, but three are
baked just right.
They did get a little wet, though.
How many cats are going to eat at the table?

9 nine

Well, those firemen have certainly
made a mess of Mother's Cat's kitchen floor.
Splish! Splosh! Splash!
They clean up with nine mops.
Five mops are red, two are green,
and two are yellow.

10 ten

Here comes Father Cat
with ten watermelons from his garden.
He slips and half of them fly out of his basket.
Five watermelons are still safe in his basket.

Who has caught the sixth, seventh,
eighth, and ninth melons?
Will Mother Cat be able to catch the tenth
one before it falls to the ground?
Look out, Mother Cat!

Now let us see what Willy has counted so far.

1 One Willy

2 Two bunnies

3 Three bunnies and three trucks

4 Four bunnies and four buses

5 Five bunnies and five racing cars

6 Six fire engines

7

Seven cats

8

Eight pies

9

Nine mops

10

Nine melons,
and the one that Mother cat caught, make ten melons.

Good for her!

11 eleven

"Now I must find some bigger numbers," says Willy. "I will look around the farm and see what I can find."

12 twelve

Farmer Cat goes into the hen house to gather eggs. He slips again and frightens his twelve hens.

Five hens are red.

Mother Cat is trying to hang
eleven shirts on the line.
Five of them blow away in the strong wind.
Then five more blow away.
But Mother Cat grabs the eleventh shirt.

Five of them are white.

And two more are black.

Twelve hens in all.
They laid twelve eggs—
one dozen eggs!
Count them yourself.

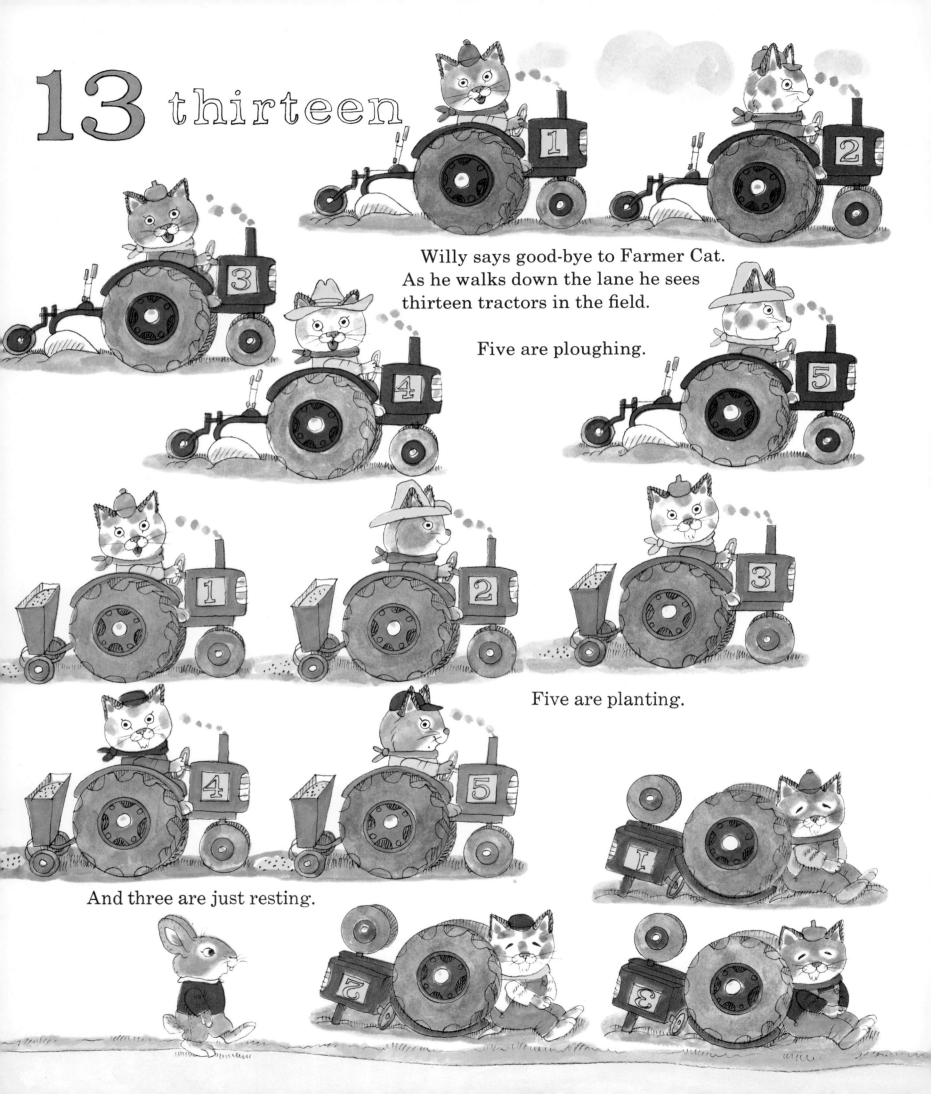

13 thirteen

Willy says good-bye to Farmer Cat. As he walks down the lane he sees thirteen tractors in the field.

Five are ploughing.

Five are planting.

And three are just resting.

14 fourteen

Suddenly Willy discovers fourteen travellers who have stopped to rest in the lane.

Five are sleeping.

Five are eating.

And four are playing a game.

Here! Here! Stop fighting over the cards, you rascals!

15 fifteen

A little farther on, Willy hears
fifteen musicians playing.

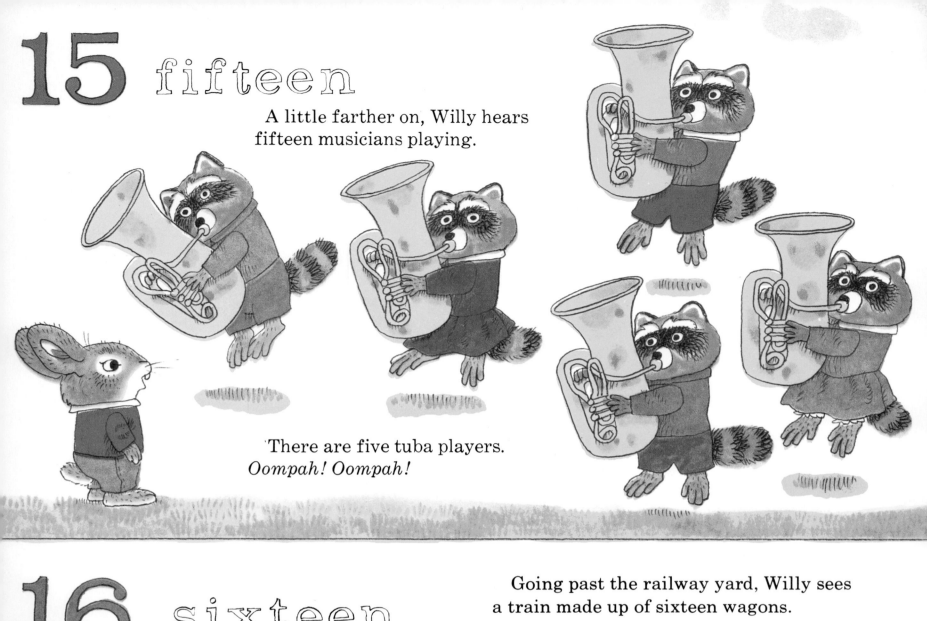

There are five tuba players.
Oompah! Oompah!

16 sixteen

Going past the railway yard, Willy sees
a train made up of sixteen wagons.

Five are box wagons.

Five are coal wagons.

Five are trumpet players. *Tootle-tee-toot!*

Can you count how many drummers there are? *Boom-da-da-boom!*

Five are petrol wagons.

And one is a guard's van.

A little engine is going
to join up to the wagons.
Do you think it can pull them all away?

17 seventeen

Suddenly seventeen aeroplanes swoop down on Willy.

Five have single wings.

Five have double wings.

18 eighteen

A long car drives by with eighteen happy lions.
There are five gentleman lions and five lady lions
sitting in the front part of the car.

Five have triple wings.

And two are jets. *Whoooosssshhh!*

Five girl lions and three boy lions
are sitting in the back of the car.
That makes eighteen happy lions in all.

19 nineteen

Willy walks up to nineteen pigs having a picnic.

20 twenty

Twenty cats are playing football. Ten cats are on each team.

Just look at that long hot dog!
Do you think it is big enough
to feed nineteen *very* hungry pigs?

Look! Number six
has just kicked a goal.

30 thirty

Willy counts thirty children
coming home from school.
He doesn't count the bus drivers.
How many bus drivers are there?

40 forty

Forty mouse cars have engine trouble.
Four transporters are taking them
to the garage to be repaired.
My Goodness! What a bumpy road!

50 fifty

As Willy walks down by the beach,
he sees fifty boats out on the ocean.

There are five barges,

five sailboats,

and five motorboats.

It looks as if one motorboat
is in trouble.

He sees five ocean liners,

five fishing boats,

five tugboats.

five police boats,

five fire boats,

and five rowing boats.

Fifty boats in all!

Hey, there, firemen!
Be careful where you
squirt that water!

60 sixty

A little farther along the beach,
Willy sees sixty frogs enjoying themselves.
How many frogs are playing ball?
How many frogs are riding in sailboats?
How many fishermen are about to fall into the water?

70 seventy

It is getting late.
On his way home, Willy stops
at the Bugs' flower garden,
where he counts seventy flowers.
Mr Bug lets Willy pick a flower
to take home to his mother.
She will be very pleased.

80 eighty

Eighty workers hurry home from work.
Some are walking. Some are riding.
One of the workers is already at his front door.
Why, it's Daddy Bunny!
Willy is greeting him at the door.

JOE'S HOT DOG FACTORY

90 ninety

At the supper table, Willy tells his father
how many things he has counted during the day.
Then the Bunny family begins to eat.
They have *ninety* carrots for supper.
My, what a hungry bunny family!
Mmmm, those carrots taste good.

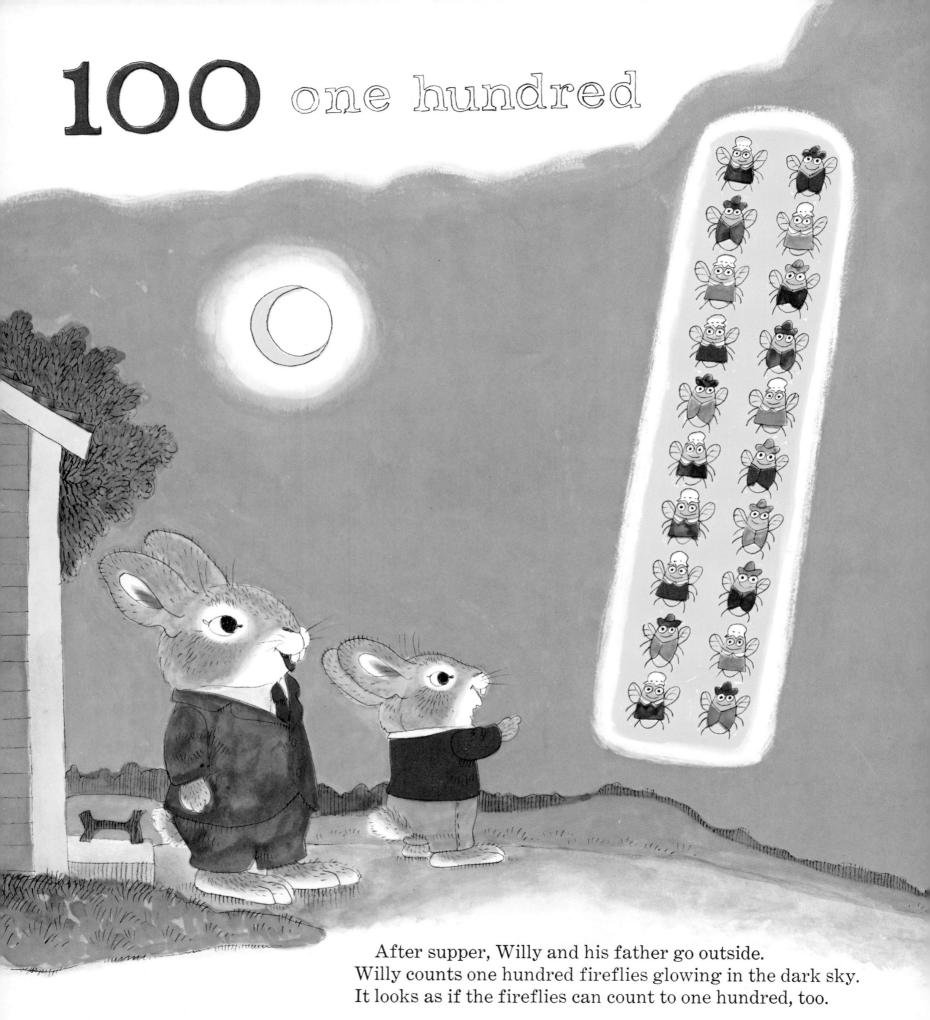

100 one hundred

After supper, Willy and his father go outside.
Willy counts one hundred fireflies glowing in the dark sky.
It looks as if the fireflies can count to one hundred, too.

And so can you!

Have you read these other books about the busy world of Richard Scarry?

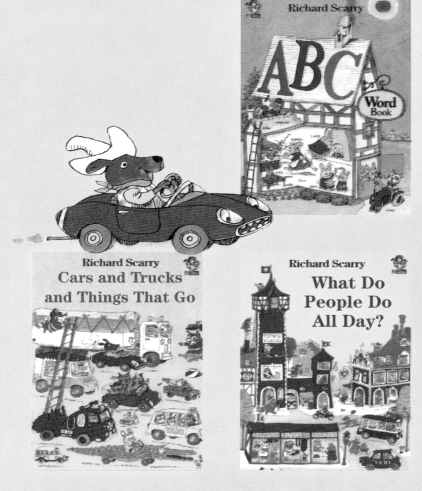

Richard Scarry
Cars and Trucks and Things That Go

Richard Scarry
What Do People Do All Day?

Richard Scarry
Best **Counting Book** Ever

Richard Scarry
Busiest People Ever

Richard Scarry
Funniest Storybook Ever

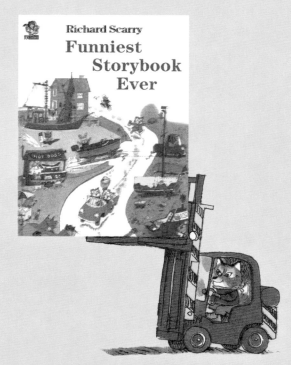